Fashion Design

Tiffany Peterson

Illustrations by David Westerfield

Heinemann Library
Chicago, Illinois

© 2003, 2008 Heinemann Library
a division of Reed Elsevier Inc.
Chicago, Illinois

Customer Service 888-454-2279
Visit our website at www.heinemannraintree.com

Designed by Jennifer Lacki and Tony Miracle
Illustrations by David Westerfield; p.28-29 illustrations by Kim Miracle
Photos by Kim Saar, p. 4; Mark Ferry, p. 5
Printed in China by Leo Paper Products Ltd.

12 11 10 09 08
10 9 8 7 6 5 4 3 2 1

New edition ISBN: 978-1-4329-1063-1 (13-digit); 1-4329-1063-9 (10-digit)

The Library of Congress has cataloged the first edition as follows:
Peterson, Tiffany.
        Fashion designs / Tiffany Peterson; illustrations by David Westerfield.
            p. cm. – (Draw it!)
Summary: Presents instructions for drawing an outfit from each decade of
the twentieth century, as well as a colonial open robe dress and a design of one's own.
Includes bibliographical references and index.
ISBN 978-1-4329-1063-1 (HC)
1. Fashion drawing–Juvenile literature. [1. Fashion drawing. 2. Drawing–Technique.]
I. Westerfield, David, 1956- ill. II. Title. III. Series.
    TT509.P48 2003
    741.6′72–dc21
                        2002015489

Acknowledgments
Cover photograph reproduced with permission of Svenja-Foto/zefa/Corbis.

Every effort has been made to contact copyright holders of any material reproduced
in this book. Any omissions will be rectified in subsequent printings if notice is given
to the publisher.

Disclaimer
All the Internet addresses (URLs) given in this book were valid at the time of going to press.
However, due to the dynamic nature of the Internet, some addresses may have changed,
or sites may have changed or ceased to exist since publication. While the author and
publisher regret any inconvenience this may cause readers, no responsibility for any such
changes can be accepted by either the author or the publisher.

Some words are shown in bold, **like this**. You can find out
what they mean by looking in the glossary.

Contents

Introduction

Would you like to improve the pictures you draw?

Well, you can! In this book, the artist has drawn some historical fashion designs. He has used lines and shapes to draw each picture in small, simple steps. Follow the steps and your picture will come together for you, too.

Here is advice from the artist:

- Always draw lightly at first.

- Draw all the shapes and pieces in the right places.

- Pay attention to the spaces between the lines as well as the lines themselves.

- Add details and **shading** to finish your drawing.

- And finally, erase the lines you don't need.

You only need a few supplies to get started.

There are just four things you need for drawing:

- a pencil (medium or soft). You might also use a fine marker or pen to finish your drawing.

- a pencil sharpener.

- paper.

- an eraser. A **kneaded eraser** works best. It can be squeezed into small or odd shapes. This eraser can also make pencil lines lighter without erasing them.

Now, are you ready? Do you have everything? Then turn the page and let's draw!

The drawings in this book were done by David Westerfield. David started drawing when he was very young. In college, he studied drawing and painting. Now he is a **commercial artist** who owns his own graphic design business. He has two children, and he likes to draw with them. David's advice to anyone who hopes to become an artist is, "practice, practice, practice—and learn as much as you can from other artists."

American Colonial Dress

The style of this dress is called open robe. The dress is like a robe worn over a full skirt. The top of the robe is kept closed by a piece of fabric called a stomacher. Stomachers have hooks on each side that connect to the inside of the robe. During the 1700s, stomachers were often decorated with bows or ruffles.

Step 1:

Start by **sketching** a big bell shape for the skirt. Draw a smaller bell shape that is upside down for the **bodice**. These are your **guidelines**.

Step 2:

Sketch one arm by drawing a shape like a banana connected to the shoulder. Draw two **vertical** lines for the hand. Add a small curved line for the curved finger. The other arm is straight. Draw two **parallel** lines from the shoulder to a point about one third down on the skirt.

Step 3:

Add an egg shape for the head. Connect it to the body by drawing two short, slightly curved lines for the neck. Add guidelines for the eyes, nose, and mouth.

Step 4:

Draw two short curved lines for the eyebrows. Below the eyebrows, draw two more short lines for the eyes. Draw a slightly curved L shape for the nose. Add a line for the mouth. Draw a curved line above one eye for the hairline. Draw a half circle on top of the head for a bun and a very small curved line for the ear. Add some curvy lines at the elbows for the ruffles of her sleeves.

Step 5:

Draw a half square for a neckline. Add ruffles to the sides of the neckline. Draw a tall V in the middle of the bodice. Draw wavy lines in the V for ruffles in the bodice. In the skirt, draw two lines from the bodice to the **hem** that are parallel to the outline. Draw lines inside the skirt to show folds in the fabric. Draw a small rounded square at the hem for a foot.

Step 6:

Erase the guidelines you no longer need. The necklace is a half circle around the neck with an oval at the bottom. Add the lower lip by drawing a short line parallel to the line you drew for the mouth. Darken the lines and add **shading** along the folds.

Civil War Dress

Like the American colonial open robe dress, this fashion of the Civil War period has a full skirt. In 1856, the "cage" **crinoline** was invented. It was a series of steel hoops connected with strips of fabric that were worn under the skirt to give it a bell shape.

Step 1:

Draw a bell shape for the skirt. Add a smaller, upside-down bell shape on top for the **bodice**. These two shapes meet at the waistline.

Step 2:

Add the arms. Draw a slanted V for the arm on the left. Draw a **vertical** line to finish the shape of the forearm. Draw a diamond shape for the hand. Draw two curved **parallel** lines from the other shoulder. Draw half of an oval for the shape of the hand.

Step 3:

Draw an oval for the head. Add two short vertical lines for the neck and short angled lines for the shoulders. Add **guidelines** for the eyes, nose, and mouth.

Step 4:

Sketch a wavy line for the ruffle on the right sleeve. Add two parallel lines around the wrists for wristbands. Add fingers to the hands. Draw a diamond shape with notches in the bottom edge for a handkerchief in the right hand. Add a wiggly line for the neckline. Add the eyebrows, eyes, and nose. Draw a line for the mouth and a short line under it. Draw the hair with short curvy lines.

Step 5:

Sketch several wavy lines across the skirt down to the bottom, or **hem**, of the skirt. Draw a V at the waistline. Add wavy lines below the neckline from one arm to the other. Sketch small wavy ovals at the middle of the wavy lines and on the right shoulder for flower **ornaments**.

Step 6:

Darken all of the lines on the skirt. Add vertical lines to the skirt to make it look ruffled. **Shade** in the top of the hair. Add shading around the bottom of the skirt for the ground.

Suffragette

At the beginning of the 1900s, women were fighting for the right to vote. As women tried to get the rights and freedoms that men had, women's fashions became more relaxed. In fact, women of this period stopped wearing **corsets**. Corsets had been used for many years to make women's waists tiny enough to fit into high-fashion dresses. A woman did not need a tiny waist to wear the dress style shown here.

Step 1:

Sketch a square that is smaller on the bottom than the top for the bodice. Under the square, sketch a bell shape for the skirt. The line between the **bodice** and the skirt is the waistline.

Step 2:

Sketch two sideways Vs for the left arm. For the right arm, draw one curved line from the top of the bodice. Add another curved line from the waistline. Sketch two sets of two **vertical** lines from the bottom of the skirt for ankles. Add curved lines for feet, with triangles for the toes. Add slight curves for heels.

Step 3:

Draw an oval for the head. Draw **guidelines** for the eyes, nose, and mouth. Add two curved lines from the neck to the shoulders and two straight lines to the collar area.

Step 4:

Draw small lines for the eyebrows, eyes, nose, and mouth. Sketch an oval around the top of the head for the **brim** of the hat. Add the top of the hat. Sketch a flower shape on the hat for an **ornament**. Draw two lines above each wrist for the sleeve cuffs. Add the hands and fingers.

Step 5:

Draw a V with a horizontal line under it for the neckline. Add two triangles for the **lapels**. Draw wavy lines around the arm guidelines for the puffy sleeves. Draw **vertical** lines from each side of the neckline down to the knee that end in **horizontal** zigzags. This is the outline of the coat. Draw two long rectangles along the inside edges of the coat.

Step 6:

Erase the guidelines you no longer need. Darken the rest of the lines. Sketch a long V with a circle at the bottom for a necklace. Add **shading** in the coat and under the chin and feet. Draw a long thin loop on the front of the shoes for decoration.

1920s Flapper

In the 1920s, skirts and dresses became shorter as hemlines went up. During this time period, women tried to look boyish. They often "bobbed" their hair, cutting it in a short style. The dresses had straight lines. Waistlines were out, but showing a lot of leg was in.

Step 1:

Sketch two wavy lines. Connect them at the top with a line that curves up for a shoulder line. Connect them at the bottom with a **horizontal** line. Draw two **parallel** horizontal lines for a belt that are higher on the left side than on the right.

Step 2:

Sketch two sideways Vs for the bent arm. Sketch a hand shape above the waistline. The other arm is hidden, but the hand rests at the hip. Sketch the hand by drawing a long triangle with a V in it for the thumb.

Step 3:

Draw two parallel **vertical** lines for the neck from the middle of the shoulder line. Add a long oval for the head. Lightly sketch a horizontal line in the oval as a **guideline** for the eyes.

Step 4:

For the leg on the right, sketch two vertical lines that slightly curve and come to a point at the bottom. Draw one long line and one shorter line for the leg on the left. To draw the sideways shoe, draw a short curved line from the bottom of the short leg line. Draw a short horizontal line for the shoe bottom. Add an upside-down V to make the heel.

Step 5:

Sketch a large V for the neckline. To draw a bow above the left hand, sketch a circle for the knot. Add two rectangles, a small one and a large one, for the bow. Draw three wavy lines across the skirt. Add shading near the chest.

Step 6:

Sketch the hair by drawing an outline close to the head. Color in the hair. Add the eyebrows, eyes, nose, and mouth. Add a long half oval for a necklace. Draw several vertical lines down the skirt for fringe. Add some **shading** on the sides of the skirt, around the armhole and above the waistline. Draw a curved line across the toes for shoes.

1930s Day Dress

Hemlines went down again in the 1930s, but not like they had been in the 1800s. Dresses of the 1930s were more elegant than the boyish straight-lined dresses of the 1920s. Dress lines were simple and showed off the shape of a woman's body. These simple lines did not include pockets, so the handbag became an important **accessory**.

Step 1:

Sketch a long shape like a curvy tube for the skirt. Add an upside-down bell shape for the **bodice**. The line where the two shapes come together is the waistline. Add a curved line across the waistline. This is the belt.

Step 2:

Sketch two sideways Vs for the arm on the left. Draw two slightly bent **parallel** lines from the right shoulder for the right arm. Draw a shape like a snake's head for the left leg. Draw a parallel line to the right of that leg. Curve the line to the left at the end. Draw a triangle on the other side of the left leg for the toes of the right foot.

Step 3:

Add two curved lines for the neck. Sketch an egg shape as a **guideline** for the head. Draw a curved line across the middle of the head. Add two triangle shapes to finish the hat's **brim**.

Step 4:

Draw a small turned L for the nose and a small sideways V for the mouth. Shade a triangle below the hat for the hair. Draw a half circle for the neckline. Draw two small curved lines at the bottom of the neck. Sketch the gloves. The top of each glove looks like the top of a heart. Add lines for the fingers. Draw a curved line across the toes for shoes.

Step 5:

Add a box inside the belt for the buckle. Add a wavy line below the belt for the bottom of the jacket. Draw wavy lines for the edges of the short sleeves. Add two shapes like the bottom of a man's necktie along the neckline. Draw a half circle under the neckline. Sketch lines inside the skirt, the bodice, and the sleeves to show folds in the fabric. Add a wavy line on the **hem**.

Step 6:

Erase the guidelines that you don't need. Add a band around the hat by drawing two curved lines. **Shade** the band and add two triangle shapes for a bow at the back of the hat. Add a curved rectangle for the purse. Color in the purse. Draw several dark curvy lines, like pleats, along the right side and bottom of the skirt. Shade the skirt, the arms, and the bodice. Shade the back of the neck. Add shading for the ground.

1940s WAC

During World War II, the Army asked women to join the Women's Army Corps (WAC) and serve in military hospitals and offices. A lot of planning went into the uniform. The jacket looked like the men's military uniform. However, many women thought it was not right to wear shorts or pants, so the WACs replaced pants with knee-length skirts.

Step 1:

Draw an upside-down bell shape with a curved bottom. Add a long **vertical** line on the right and a long curved line on the left. Connect the two lines with a **horizontal** line at the bottom for a skirt. The curved line across the middle is the waistline.

Step 2:

Sketch two sideways Vs for each arm. Add the shape of a curved hand on the right. Draw a line curving down from the right bottom of the skirt for a leg. Add a curved line for the inside of the leg and heel of the shoe. Add the bottom of the shoe. Draw two slightly curved lines for the leg on the left. Make the left line slightly curve out. Connect the two lines with a curve.

Step 3:

Add two short vertical lines for the neck and an oval for the head. Lightly sketch **guidelines** for the eyes, nose, and mouth.

Step 4:

Sketch a tilted square on top of the head for the hat. Add curly hair by drawing wavy lines around the face. Add the eyebrows, eyes, nose, and mouth. Draw a small V close to the neck for the neckline. Sketch a finger for the hand on the left. Draw a square with a line across it for the handbag. Draw two **parallel** lines across the wrists for the jacket cuffs. Draw two lines across the left shoe and a line across the right foot.

Step 5:

Draw two sideways Ms on either side of the neck for the **lapels**. Add an X for the tie. Draw an upside-down V at the top of the X to connect the lines. Draw a wavy line from the lapels to the waistline. Add two square pockets and a waistband to the jacket. Draw two long lines from the shoulder to the belt, and two short lines from the back corner of the bag to the arm for the bag straps. Add an oval and a circle for the clasp of the bag. **Shade** the middle of the skirt.

Step 6:

Erase guidelines that you don't need and darken the rest. Add a square on the hat with a vertical line through the center for bars. Add two vertical lines to the pockets and draw buttons. Add a patch on the right arm. Color the purse, leaving parts of it white so it looks glossy. Color the shoes, jacket, hair, and hat. Add shading to the left sides of the legs.

1950s Dior

Christian Dior created a style called the New Look. Dior dresses had broad shoulders, a small waist, and full hips. Women again wore layered **petticoats** to create full skirts. Luckily, in the 1950s, petticoats were no longer made of heavy cotton. They were made of light netting.

Step 1:

Sketch a bell shape for the skirt. Be sure to leave room for the legs and feet underneath. Draw a smaller upside-down bell shape for the **bodice**. Darken the line between the skirt and the bodice to show the waistline.

Step 2:

Add the right arm by drawing two **parallel** lines from the right shoulder. Sketch the hand by adding two curved lines from the bottom of the arm. Draw two more lines from the left shoulder. Add a round shape for the hand. Draw one straight leg from the center of the skirt. Add several curved lines as a **guideline** for a high-heeled shoe. Draw the second leg and shoe at an angle.

Step 3:

Draw two curved lines for the neck. Add a pointed oval for the head. Draw dashes for guidelines for the mouth, nose, and eyes.

Step 4:

Draw the nose, mouth, eyebrow, and eye. Draw a wavy line from the forehead to the top of the neck for the hair. Finish the hair by drawing a curved line from the neck to the back of the head. Sketch a curvy oval for the hat. Draw curved lines across the elbows of the arms for the tops of the gloves. Sketch the fingers. Add curved lines above the toes for the shoes.

Step 5:

Make the armholes of the sleeveless dress by drawing curved lines from the tops of the shoulders to the sides of the bodice. Draw a wide V for the neckline. Continue the left side of the V to the waistline. Add a wide belt, or sash, by drawing two curved parallel lines at the waistline. Draw several dark **vertical** lines from the sash for folds.

Step 6:

Erase the guidelines that you don't need. Draw several **horizontal** lines along the gloves for folds. **Shade** the fabric of the dress to show folds. Shade the ground and then the neck under the chin and the tops of the legs for shadow.

1960s Minidress

1960s youths **rebelled** against the styles of the 1950s. Women's hairstyles got shorter, and so did their dresses. Dresses in the 1960s became so short, in fact, they were called minidresses. Clothes in the 1960s were often made with bright colors and bold patterns.

Step 1:

Sketch a rectangle with curvy sides.

Step 2:

Sketch two backwards 7s for the arm on the left. Sketch a long, thin rectangle for the leg on the right. Add the rough shape of the foot at the bottom by drawing a line that angles out. Draw another rectangle at an angle for the leg on the left. Add the foot by drawing an angled V.

Step 3:

Sketch a pointed oval for the head. Add two lines for the neck. Add a curl at the back of the jaw line for the ear. At the bottom of the neck, draw a short, slanted line. Sketch two **horizontal** lines as **guidelines** for the eyes and nose.

Step 4:

Draw several lines for the hair along the forehead. Draw the eyebrow, eye, nose, and mouth. Draw a circle for a large hoop earring. Add the hand and the three fingers that show. Draw a line across each leg just below the knee for the tops of the boots. Sketch in short lines for knees. Darken the lines for the boots and add a heel to the right boot with a small rectangle.

Step 5:

Sketch a curved line for the neckline and a J for the armhole on the left. Draw a line from near the bottom of the armhole across the dress. Add two rounded lines at the right side of the dress to show the shoulder and hand of the hidden arm. Sketch a shape like a stop sign on the dress near the hand. Draw lines coming out from each corner of the stop sign shape.

Step 6:

Erase the guidelines that you do not need. Darken the lines in the picture. **Shade** the hair. Color in the dress. Add some shading around the feet for the ground. Shade the legs so they look different from the boots.

1970s Pantsuit

Women have worn pants for decades. In the 1970s, women could wear pants and pantsuits to dressy and formal events for the first time. The shoes in this drawing are called platform shoes. They were very popular in the 1970s.

Step 1:

Sketch two ovals on top of each other.

Step 2:

Connect the circles with two curved lines. Add a slightly pointed oval for the head. Sketch three **horizontal guidelines** for the eyes, nose, and mouth. Add two short curved lines for the neck.

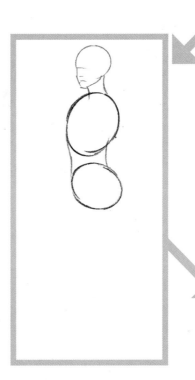

Step 3:

Draw two sideways Vs for the right arm. Add slightly bent **vertical** lines for the left arm. Draw two long vertical lines for the leg on the right. Make the left line curve out at the end. Sketch a rectangle for the foot. Draw two sideways Vs for the leg on the left. Sketch half of a slanted rectangle for the toe of the shoe. Add a line for the back of the heel.

Step 4:

Draw two Vs for the collar. Sketch two curved lines across the waist for the belt. Add a small square for the belt buckle. Add a line from the collar to the waist and short curvy lines around the left arm for the sleeve. Draw a line across the upper part of the left leg and an upside-down V for the bottom of the jacket. Draw a curved line across the top of the right shoe for the pant cuff. Add a curved line from the toe area to the cuff on both shoes. Sketch a small rectangle for the heels.

Step 5:

Draw a curved line along the top and back of the head. Add jagged lines along the forehead and side of the face for hair. Make a V below the chin on the right to outline the neck. Draw a small sideways V under the chin on the left for hair. Add eyes, eyebrows, mouth, and a curved L shape for the nose. Draw a rectangle for the right hand and wrist. Draw the left hand with little Us and Vs for fingers.

Step 6:

Erase guidelines that you do not need. Draw two lines across each wrist for the sleeve cuffs. Add curvy lines along the edges of the sleeves and legs to show folds in the fabric. Color the hair. Darken the lines of the drawing. **Shade** the ground around her feet.

1980s Mini-Crini

In the 1980s, the "mini-crini" appeared. It was a shorter version of the **crinolined** dresses that were popular in the 1950s. The designer added two puffs at the hips to make the woman's hips look wider and her waist look smaller.

Step 1:

Draw a bell shape with a curved rectangle on top of it. This is the **guideline** for the dress.

Step 2:

Sketch a short **vertical** line along the right side of the **bodice** for the arm on the right. Draw a curvy backwards L from the top of the left shoulder. Sketch another backwards L under it to finish the left arm. Add the rough shape of the left hand. Draw two long, curvy lines for the leg on the left. Draw a long L for the leg on the right.

Step 3:

Sketch a pointed oval for the head. Draw a short guideline for the eyes. Draw a short line on the left and a longer curved line on the right for the neck.

Step 4:

Sketch the hair by drawing a rough triangle on top of the head. On both sides of the face, add some wiggly lines for curls and waves. Draw the eyebrows, eyes, nose, and mouth. Put a small line on the cheek for a cheekbone. Add fingers by drawing tiny Vs.

Step 5:

Add an upside-down V across each of the feet for the tops of the shoes. For the puffs at the waist sketch a sideways 8 with straight lines. Draw a wide M for the top of the dress. Draw a line down the front of the dress. Add some lines along the sides of the bodice to show folds in the fabric.

Step 6:

Darken all of the lines. Add **shading** to the right arm, the top half of the left arm, and on the tops of the legs.

1990s Formal Gown

In the 1990s, fashion designers looked to the past for ideas. Styles from the 50s, 60s, and 70s came back. Women had many choices in the 1990s. Everything from the minidress to the full-length gown was stylish. This full-length dress borrows from the fashions of the 1970s.

Step 1:

Sketch the skirt by drawing a long triangle with no top point. Add an upside-down bell shape on top for the **bodice**.

Step 2:

Draw a long **vertical** line from the right shoulder down to the skirt. Add a shorter **parallel** line to finish the **guideline** for the right arm. Draw a tipped L shape starting at the left shoulder. Add a smaller L shape for the rest of the left arm.

Step 3:

Sketch a slightly pointed oval for the head. Connect it to the body by drawing two curved lines for the neck. Sketch two **horizontal** lines as guidelines for the eyes and mouth.

Step 4:

Draw the nose, mouth, and eye. Add a curved line for the eyebrow. Draw a backwards C for an ear and a tiny circle for an earring. Sketch several horizontal lines from the forehead toward the back of the head for the hair. Add curly hair in the back by drawing two ovals with lines in them at the back of the head. Draw four curved fingers at the waist. Draw a horizontal line across the right wrist for the bottom of the sleeve.

Step 5:

Sketch half of a square with rounded corners for the dress's neckline. Draw six wavy lines across the skirt to create a pattern of wide cloud-like stripes. Sketch several vertical lines in the bottom half of the skirt for folds in the fabric. Add a curvy line at the bottom of the skirt for the hemline.

Step 6:

Erase the guidelines that you do not need. Darken all of the lines. Add **shading** at the back of the neck and under the chin. Color in the bodice and sleeves of the dress. Color in the stripes in the skirt. Add some shading for the ground.

Fashion in the Year 2000

In the year 2000, fashion became very casual. Styles were much more comfortable than those from earlier decades. Women and men wore jeans more often, and all different kinds of sneakers were very popular.

Step 1:

Draw a large triangle over an oval.

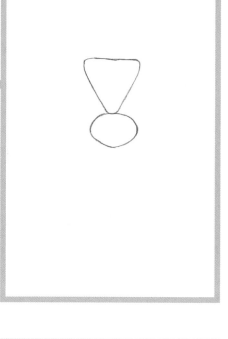

Step 2:

Draw an oval over the triangle for the head. Add curved lines for the eyes, nose, and mouth. Draw two curved lines under the oval for the neck. Draw two curved lines from the top corners of the triangle for the waist.

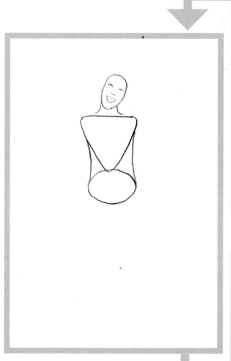

Step 3:

Draw two wide Vs as **guidelines** for the arms. Draw two lines for guidelines for the legs. Add circles for the knees. Draw curved Vs for the shoes.

Step 4:

Sketch the jacket by drawing two tall rectangles with tilted tops. Draw wide Vs above your arm guidelines for the top of the sleeves. For the rest of the sleeves, draw two Vs below your arm guidelines. For the pants, draw two tall rectangles that intersect in a V. Add hands by drawing curved rectangles with rounded triangles for fingers.

Step 5:

Sketch a wavy circle around the head for the hair. Add two curved lines for eyebrows, and fill in the lips. Sketch the shirt by adding a curved line below the neck and another above the top of the pants.

Step 6:

Erase the guidelines that you don't need. **Shade** the jeans and jacket darkest around the edges and lightest in the center. Add a necklace by drawing a dark curved line with a triangle in the middle. Add dark lines on the jeans and t-shirt to show folds.

Create Your Own Fashion Design

You can sketch this figure, or human shape, and add clothes to it. Look back through the designs in this book for ideas or create something completely new. Use your imagination and have fun!

Step 1:

Draw a **vertical** oval over a smaller oval.

Step 2:

Sketch a small oval for the head. Add a curved L shape for the face and chin. Draw a vertical line at the end of the L shape for the jawline. Add two vertical lines for the neck. Lightly sketch three **horizontal** lines as **guidelines** for the eyes, nose, and mouth.

Step 3:

Draw the arms and legs using guidelines. Add circles to show the knees.

Step 4:

Sketch the shape of the body by drawing lines connecting the guideline circles. Draw a line across the shoulders.

Step 5:

Draw the hands and feet. Sketch the hair in any style you want. Add a curved L shape for a nose. Draw two curved lines for the mouth. Add eyes and eyebrows.

Step 6:

Now, add your own fashion design. Sketch the clothes lightly at first. Then erase the guidelines you do not need and darken the lines of the final drawing.

Glossary/Art Glossary

accessory extra piece of clothing or jewelry worn with an outfit

bars in a military uniform, bars made of metal show the rank, or position, of the person wearing them

bodice top half of a dress

brim edge of a hat that sticks out

commercial artist person who designs and illustrates things for other people

corset piece of clothing worn under a dress to make a woman's waist look smaller

crinoline stiff underskirt worn to make a dress look fuller

hem bottom edge of a skirt or dress

lapels two parts of a jacket or shirt that fold back from the neckline

ornament something that is added as decoration

petticoat full, often ruffled, underskirt worn to make a dress look fuller

rebel to go against

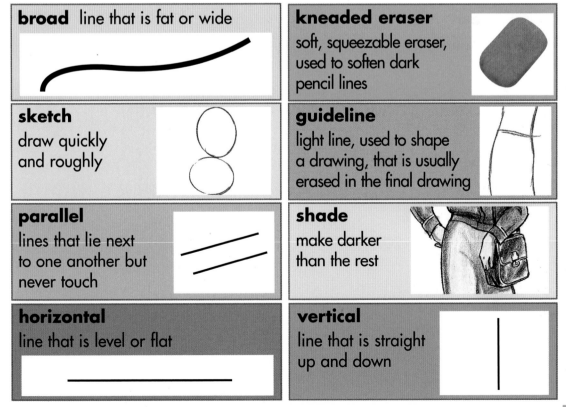

broad line that is fat or wide

sketch draw quickly and roughly

parallel lines that lie next to one another but never touch

horizontal line that is level or flat

kneaded eraser soft, squeezable eraser, used to soften dark pencil lines

guideline light line, used to shape a drawing, that is usually erased in the final drawing

shade make darker than the rest

vertical line that is straight up and down

More Books to Read

Books about Drawing

Dickens, Rosie. *Drawing Faces*. Tulsa, Oklahoma: EDC Publishing, 2004.

Hart, Christopher. *How to Draw Chic Fashions*. Englewood Cliffs, New Jersey: Loew-Cornell, Inc., 2006.

Books about Fashion

Reynolds, Helen. *A Fashionable History of Dresses and Skirts*. Chicago: Raintree, 2003.

Rivera, Ursula. *Fashion*. New York: Scholastic, 2004.

Index